DARK MATTERS

Nature's Reaction to Light Pollution

JOAN MARIE GALAT

Red Deer Press

For Mom, who was right
to remind me to turn off the lights.

———————

The author acknowledges the Canada Council
for the Arts for its much appreciated financial
support during the research and writing of
Dark Matters – Nature's Reaction to Light Pollution

Published in Canada by Red Deer Press,
195 Allstate Parkway, Markham, Ontario L3R 4T8

All inquiries should be addressed to Red Deer Press,
195 Allstate Parkway, Markham, Ontario L3R 4T8.
reddeerpress.com

10 9 8 7 6 5 4 3 2 1

Red Deer Press acknowledges with thanks the Canada Council
for the Arts, and the Ontario Arts Council for their support of our
publishing program. We acknowledge the financial support of
the Government of Canada through the Canada Book Fund (CBF)
for our publishing activities.

ONTARIO ARTS COUNCIL
CONSEIL DES ARTS DE L'ONTARIO
an Ontario government agency
un organisme du gouvernement de l'Ontario

Canada Council   Conseil des arts
for the Arts   du Canada

Library and Archives Canada Cataloguing in Publication
Galat, Joan Marie, 1963-, author
Dark matters / Joan Marie Galat.

ISBN 978-0-88995-515-8 (paperback)

1. Light pollution--Juvenile literature. I. Title.

QB51.3.L53 G34 2017   j522   C2017-902888-1

Published in the United States in 2017 by Red Deer Press,
311 Washington Street, Brighton, Massachusetts 02135

Publisher Cataloging-in-Publication Data (U.S)
Galat, Joan Marie, 1963-, author
Dark matters / Joan Marie Galat.

ISBN 978-0-88995-515-8 (paperback)

1. Light pollution--Juvenile literature. I. Title.

QB51.3.L53 G34 2017   j522   C2014-902888-1

Names: Galat, Joan Marie, 1963-, author.
Title: Dark matters / Joan Galat.
Description: Toronto, Ontario Canada : Red Deer Press, 2017. |
Summary: "Dark Matters introduces readers
to the causes and harmful effects of light pollution.
The book contains facts and illustrations,
as well as tips and suggestions on how young people
can reduce light pollution"– Provided by publisher.
Identifiers: ISBN 978-0-88995-515-8 (pbk.)
Subjects: LCSH: Light pollution – Juvenile literature. | BISAC:
JUVENILE NONFICTION /Science & Nature / Environmental
Conservation & Protection.
Classification: LCC QB51.3.L53G353 | DDC 363.7 – dc23

Edited for the Press by Peter Carver
Design by Tanya Montini
Printed by Regent, China

Contents

Looking Up

Lying on my back in three feet of snow, I gaze up at the night sky and look for constellations—pictures in the stars. I think I find the Big Dipper. Pointing my mitten north, I count the stars up to seven. The Big Dipper forms part of a constellation called the Big Bear. But how can a giant soup spoon shaped out of stars represent a bear? Many years pass before I find the answer to that question.

Three things interest me in the night sky—playing outside in the dark, the *How and Why Book of Astronomy*, and staring out car windows on long nighttime drives. The Sun sets early in the fall and winter where I live in Canada—near Edmonton, the second largest city in Alberta. It's dark by 5:00 PM in the months before and after Christmas. But that's too early to stop playing. Under a streetlight, I push and pile the front yard snow. When my fort is built, I step inside and lie on my back.

My down-fill jacket and snow pants keep me warm. The snowy fort walls stop the wind. In fact, I'm so warm I lick snowflakes

TOO MANY LIGHTS
Light pollution exists when unwanted light is present. It is caused when people use too many lights or poorly designed light fixtures.

from my mitten. One wall is just high enough to block the light from the street lamp.

I can still see the red light on the CBC tower. Its flashing beam warns airplanes not to fly too close. It reminds me of a light I used to notice when we lived in Maryland when I was only seven. We didn't get much snow there, but I remember being outside at night and seeing the bright white beam of an airport beacon sweep the sky to lead pilots to the airport.

I line myself up along the snow wall and look straight up. The stars spread out like bits of sparkling glitter on a black blanket. The longer I look, the more stars I can make out. How can I not wonder what's out there? I try to make out different colored stars. Maybe I'm looking at a planet and don't even know it. A shooting star streaks across the sky. I make a wish in case that might be lucky.

With the Sun long gone, the temperature drops. The scarf around my neck is loose and winter air chills my skin. I wade through snowdrifts and open the back door. Light pours into my face. It makes my eyes squint into slits as I drop my mitts and boots on the heat register to dry. My glasses fog up.

Mom makes me hot chocolate. Between sips, I flip through my astronomy book and try to figure out what I have seen. Was that a red star or Mars? What are those dark spots on the Moon? How do I know when I've found a constellation? I won't allow myself to believe that I have really found one unless I'm certain I've spotted each one of the stars on my sky map. I don't yet know that streetlights and houselights make dim stars hard to see.

STARGAZING FROM THE PUMPKIN

The next time I get the chance to stargaze, I'm under a patchwork blanket in the back seat of a car. Every couple of months we drive from our home in Sherwood Park to St. Paul, a small town in northeastern Alberta. We go to visit Mom's family for the day. Dad named the car "the Pumpkin" because it is bright orange. The entire backseat of the Pumpkin is mine. My teenage sisters don't like long driving trips. They say they would rather be with their friends. I think they're embarrassed to be seen in the Pumpkin. Even though I'm ten, I'm still the youngest. So I have to go—but I don't really mind. I usually read for most of the two-hour drive. We always stop for candy along the way. I pick raspberry drops or Scotch mints.

It's usually late when we leave for home and, on the way, I sprawl across the backseat, sucking on my candy if there's any left. It's too dark to read. Sometimes I scoot back and forth between the windows to see different parts of the sky. This is in the early seventies—before wearing seatbelts became the law.

It is long past my normal bedtime. I gaze into the sky. There is nothing else to do. It will be more than thirty years before cars have DVD players or kids have MP3 players. Hand-held computer games aren't invented yet. No one has smart phones. Most cars don't even have FM radio. And the station my parents listen to is boring— talk, talk, talk! I search for constellations.

In the countryside, land and sky blend into the darkest black. Sometimes yard lights on farms or headlights from traffic cast white shapes. On moonlit nights, when the weather is cloudy and windy, I watch the Moon disappear and reappear from behind the clouds. When there's no Moon, I can see the Milky Way—our very own galaxy. It looks like a pathway of light through the sky. It's dark enough for me to make out the place where the galaxy separates into two roadways of light.

If we're lucky, the northern lights dance across the sky. They are also called the "Aurora Borealis." Auroras are white, yellow, and green. Sometimes shades of purple and blue or tinges of pink or red appear. My parents look up, too. They like watching the glowing lights dip and turn and change shape.

I love the northern lights but I want to find the constellations. I look for Orion the Hunter.

Taurus, the Bull; and Draco, the Dragon. People from ancient cultures imagined constellations more than six thousand years ago. I think it's cool to look up and see the same pictures in the sky as the people who lived on Earth so long ago. I know that constellations are more than fun. They are important. Astronomers use them to form a map of the sky. If you want to look for a planet, you need to know where to look on the sky map.

As we approach Vegreville, a small town known for its gigantic Ukrainian Easter Egg, I notice an eerie orange glow in the sky. Far away it looks like a sunrise or sunset, but I know it is the wrong time of night for either one. I imagine the giant egg has hatched an alien being. It glimmers over the entire town, casting a neon spell, making young children howl like coyotes at the Moon. I weave a story inside my head until we get closer and I realize the orange glow is caused by lights in the town. Closer to home, Edmonton's glow grows even brighter. We can see it from fifty kilometers away. Turning lights on after sunset must make people feel safer. I wonder if everyone in towns and cities is afraid of the dark and stare into the night until I fall asleep. In the morning I wake up in my own bed. Dad must have carried me in.

A PLACE OF WONDER

People in ancient cultures looked up at a black velvet sky that glittered with starlight. More than six thousand years ago, they imagined pictures shaped out of stars and named the first constellations. They saw objects that seemed to wander the cosmos and named the planets.

The night sky has always held a special place of wonder for people who gazed up at its majesty. Early cave dwellers carved starry pictures on the walls of their homes. In the north and south, people watched the dancing auroras. They imagined their ancestors crossing to the heavens along the starry path of the Milky Way.

SKY GLOW VS. NATURAL LIGHT

Astronomical light pollution occurs when unwanted light makes it hard to see objects in the night sky. When you see an orange glow over distant towns and cities, the pollution is called sky glow. Natural light adds to sky glow and can also interfere with stargazing.

Natural light includes:

* auroras
* starlight
* sunlight that reflects off the Moon and Earth
* nebulae-clouds of dust and gas in space, and
* Zodiac light, created when sunlight reflects off interplanetary dust.

WAVELENGTHS
Wavelengths of ordinary light vibrate in many different directions as they travel; this creates unpolarized light. When many wavelengths vibrate horizontally, polarized light forms and appears to humans as glare. Light can become polarized and creates daytime light pollution when it reflects off objects like water, sand, metal, or asphalt roads.

WHAT EXACTLY IS LIGHT?

You know light helps you see, but what exactly is it? Light is a form of energy—a type of electromagnetic radiation that travels in vibrating waves. It is made up of billions of tiny particles called photons. Individual photons are too small to see and have no mass, so they travel very quickly. If you were made of light, you could travel 186,000 miles (300,000 kilometers) per second.

Radiation you can see is called visible light. When you view an object's color, you are seeing an individual wavelength of reflected light. The other colors have been absorbed. The longest wavelengths you can see are red; the shortest are blue. White light is a mixture of all the colors of the rainbow, which always appear in the same order: red – orange – yellow – green – blue – indigo – violet. Other kinds of light have wavelengths too short or too long for human eyes to see. These include X-rays, microwaves, radio and television waves, gamma rays, ultraviolet light, and infrared light.

You feel radiation when you sense heat from the Sun, a hot candle flame, or a warm towel from the dryer. The energy you feel comes from invisible infrared light. Plants and some animal species react to light humans cannot see. Bees detect ultraviolet light patterns reflected by flowers. This helps them locate the nectar they need. Ants use polarized light as a compass. Rattlesnakes and other members of the pit viper family find warm-blooded prey by responding to infrared light.

Pigeons see polarized light patterns that are invisible to humans and use them to help navigate. Dragonflies and mayflies are attracted to polarized light because it fools them into thinking that they are flying over a body of water where they can feed and breed. Species that mistake a road for water may try to defend the territory and be hit by cars. They may even lay eggs on the road—a place where they cannot survive.

Neighborhood Lights

Often on a Friday night, Mom goes to Safeway to get groceries. She says she likes to shop at night because that's when she has the most energy. Mom calls herself a night owl. Sometimes I go with her and hang out in the mall while she shops. I bring the money I earn polishing Dad's stinky shoes.

Before we leave, Mom asks me to walk the dog, so I pull on my jacket and sneakers and rattle the leash. Our beagle comes running and nearly knocks me over, but I get the leash hooked onto his collar and off we go. It's a sniff-a-thon for Ringo, and I try to be patient as he thoroughly inspects the base of every streetlight along the way.

While I wait, my fingers feel a gumball in my pocket and I pop it in my mouth. I'm attempting my specialty—a bubble, inside a bubble, inside a bubble—when I notice something weird at a

house up the street. It's too dark to make out from where I stand, but it looks like a small boxy car parked right on someone's lawn. Shadows the size of fire hydrants rise up around it. I know this neighborhood, and whatever I'm seeing—it's not usually here.

Ringo knows it, too. A deep growl starts low in his throat. Before I can grip the leash more tightly, he yanks his head and the loop slides from my hand. Ringo takes off at a full-speed gallop, barking like he means business. I race after him, but stop short when someone flicks a switch and light fills the yard.

For a moment, I'm blinded. I can hear Ringo barking but I can't see him. Then my eyes adjust and the car on the grass becomes Santa in a sleigh. The fire hydrants are elves carrying gift-wrapped boxes. Ringo is facing down a reindeer made of hundreds of tiny white lights and one ruby-red blinking nose. He lets out a stream of yaps with every reindeer nose blink. Across the sidewalk, golden yellow lights outline a nativity scene sheltering Jesus in a manger. I make my way around statues of the Three Wise Men lit with floodlights, grab Ringo's leash, and coax him back to the street. "You don't need to protect me from Rudolph," I tell him.

A man comes around the side of the house and tells me, "Just testing the lights. I guess your dog doesn't have the Christmas spirit." I'm thinking Christmas is nearly two months away but I just mutter, "Sorry," and pull Ringo toward home.

I tell Mom, who's sitting in the car ready to go to the mall, what happened. She says some people on the prairies like to get their lights set up before winter really hits. Wow. I can't believe it. Christmas lights before Halloween.

We pull into the parking lot where glowing neon signs advertise the name of each store. Car headlights sweep across the lot as drivers circle to find parking spots near an entrance. Mom has to pull the sun visor down when a truck's bright lights nearly blind her. We park beneath a light that is bright enough to cast dark shadows.

I hear honking as we walk toward the glass-door entrance but it's not from a car. Canada geese fly overhead. It's the fall migration. I wonder where they're going and where they've been. How do they decide where to stop? I look way up, but the glare is too bright for me to see the birds or the stars. Instead, I notice men on ladders, stringing armloads of Christmas lights across a storefront. I guess they're taking advantage of the mild weather, too.

Safeway is at one end of the mall, Zeller's at the other. Only two places in between interest me—the food kiosk and the toy store. I swallow my gum, buy a malt, and head for the toys. Almost every item costs more than the coins in my pocket but I don't care. I'm not especially longing for anything. I just like to look. Wandering past the board games, puzzles, dolls, and action figures, I stop at the books. Each title is displayed cover out. One is illustrated with bright-colored birds. I wonder if I can find out where the geese are going. First, I have to get rid of my empty malt cup. I dash into the mall, toss it into the trash bin, and return to the book display. After I inspect the book to make sure it's not bent or damaged in any way, I carry it to the cashier.

I try to read in the car on the way home but it's too dark. Or is it? Every time we pass under a streetlight, enough light shines on the page for me to read a sentence or two. My eyes try to adjust to light, then dark, then light again. It's too frustrating, so I give up. Back home, I sit at the kitchen table, open the book, and hold the pages up to my nose. New-book-smell gives me a feeling that's hard to describe. It's a bit like hope and certainty at the same time. Flipping through the pages, I discover owls are adapted to nighttime living. Rough-edged flight feathers allow them to soar through the sky without making a sound. Silent flight and big eyes make them fantastic nighttime hunters. I think I wouldn't mind being an owl and

GLARE!
Glare from artificial light can create dangerous situations when it temporarily blinds pedestrians, drivers, and cyclists. Bright headlights that shine into drivers' eyes cause fatigue and stress. This can lead to driving errors and accidents.

being able to see at night, but then I think, "Ugh, who wants to eat mice?"

I like knowing facts and keep reading. My friends think this hobby is strange but I still want to know everything—why some birds are nocturnal, why they migrate at night, and what they need to survive. I become so intrigued that I begin to collect books about birds. Now I like to visit a third store in the mall—the bookstore.

TYPES OF LIGHT POLLUTION

Have you ever felt light in your eyes? Lights cause different types of problems called glare, light trespass, sky glow, over-illumination, and clutter. A light may cause pollution in more than one category.

Light trespass is light that goes where it is not wanted or needed. A streetlight that shines into your bedroom window is light trespass. It can make it hard for you to sleep.

Over-illumination is the use of more lights and brighter lights than needed. Imagine a building where a single light switch controls the lights in every room. It would be impossible to turn off unneeded lights. Over-illumination would occur. The same thing happens when lights are left on in a classroom even when sunshine brightens the room.

Clutter describes groups of lights that are larger than needed. You see clutter on roads that have lots of brightly lit advertising and poorly designed streetlights. Clutter can distract drivers and pedestrians.

Sea Turtles

In school, Mr. Nestransky writes about four types of pollution on the blackboard—air pollution, noise pollution, land pollution, and water pollution. He tells us to write a report on one of the pollutions, so I pick water.

On Saturday, I ride my bike to the public library to do my research. I especially want to know how animals are affected by water pollution. I collect the books I need for my report, then wander over to see what's going on in the presentation room. An author is talking about her book on sea turtles. A librarian waves me to come in, so I take a chair in the back.

The author is explaining how sea turtles almost always lay their eggs at night to avoid daytime predators. A female slowly crawls out of the ocean and makes her way up a remote sandy beach. The turtle digs a hole, drops

Unlike land turtles, sea turtles can't hide their heads and legs inside the shell. That makes them more vulnerable when they come in contact with predators.

Green turtle laying eggs.

her eggs, and covers them with dry sand. She returns to the sea—never returning to the nest.

At the end of the talk, we're allowed to ask questions. I'm a bit nervous about speaking out in front of strangers but I really want to know something. Biting my bottom lip, I raise my hand. She probably won't notice me back here anyway.

But she does!

Uh-oh! I've been thinking about my question instead of listening to what other people asked. What if someone else has already asked my question? I can feel my face turning pink. The author waits and the people in the rows ahead twist back to look at me. I blurt out my question. "Do sea turtles have problems because of water pollution?"

"Absolutely!" she says, "I meant to bring that up." The author explains that leatherback sea turtles often mistake floating plastic bags for jellyfish—a main part of their diet. Plastic onion bags, balloons, and food wrappers are problems, too. Turtles may get tangled in rope and fishing line that's been lost in the ocean.

The author passes around a picture that shows a turtle eating a plastic bag and explains that litter can block a turtle's intestine and cause starvation. Then she points out that sea turtles have lived on Earth more than 100 million years. They survived even when dinosaurs became extinct! But now all seven species of sea turtle struggle to survive.

Hearing about animals suffering makes me uncomfortable. Seeing the picture puts my stomach in knots. I'm disgusted with the way people treat our planet. I feel sorry for fish and birds and other animals. I wonder how these problems can be fixed.

WHY CARE ABOUT SEA TURTLES?

Sea turtles spend more than ninety percent of their lives in water, yet they affect both beach and ocean ecosystems. On land, sea turtles impact the environment by laying many eggs that never hatch. Unhatched eggs add nutrients to sand and help make it possible for plants to grow and be healthy. The roots of the plants, in turn, prevent sand from blowing away. Plants are important in helping hold sand dunes together.

In the ocean, some turtle species feed on sea grass, a plant that grows continually, just like grass on a lawn. Sea grass provides important habitat for many ocean creatures, including fish, octopus, squid, oysters, shrimp, and clams. Grazing sea turtles keep the grass short and healthy. They also eat seaweed, coral, and sponge. Sea turtles prevent these species from growing too much and choking out other forms of life. Marine turtles are needed to ensure these habitats do not disappear. Lost habitat could eventually affect commercial fish species that are important to humans, and vital members of the food chain.

NESTING SEA TURTLES

While male turtles rarely come to shore after birth, female turtles lay their eggs on remote sandy beaches. Scientists have noticed some beaches may be used by thousands of turtles, while similar beaches are much less popular. Most sea turtle species lay their eggs on the same beach year after year, often within a few hundred yards of last year's nest. Unfortunately, resorts, homes, and businesses are built on beaches that once provided natural habitat. These nesting sites were ideal in past centuries when nights were dark, but today's turtles must cope with artificial light.

Females almost always lay their eggs at night to help them avoid land-living predators that are diurnal—active during the day. Nesting sea turtles slowly crawl out of the ocean and make their way up the beach. After reaching dry sand, the turtle digs a hole. Depending on the species, females drop from 80 to 120 eggs. They cover the egg chamber with sand and hide the nest by scattering more sand over the area. After nesting, females return to the sea. They never go back to the nest.

Light pollution can cause baby sea turtle hatchlings to lose direction.

Nesting turtles stop often, sometimes turning around and going back into the ocean without nesting. This behavior is called a "false crawl." Turtles will give up building a nest at their chosen location if they have too many false crawls. Instead, they may drop their eggs in the water or choose a poor spot to nest, such as the wetter, cooler sand closer to the ocean where waves still reach.

Scientists are still exploring all the reasons false crawls occur. However, they do know artificial lighting, as well as seeing people on the beach, can trigger false crawls. Sky glow and lights that are directly visible take away the darkness that sea turtles need to nest. Fewer turtles nest on beaches with a lot of artificial light. And fewer hatchlings survive when artificial lighting causes too many turtles to nest close together. Lights also impact the coastal sea habitats that provide turtles with important feeding areas.

HATCHLINGS NEED WATER

Turtle eggs hatch at night or during rain showers when the weather is cool. Newborn turtles break out of their shells and erupt from the nest as a group. The hatchlings find their way to the ocean in an act called "seafinding." This inborn urge causes them to make their way toward the brightest horizon. They move across the sand as quickly as they can.

Under natural conditions, the brightest area is the ocean—lit by the reflections of the Moon and stars. Even when the Moon is not visible, young turtles still scramble toward the water. They may have an inborn tendency to move away from dark silhouettes, such as the shapes and shadows of sand dunes and plants.

When light pollution is present, hatchling turtles become confused. The more direct light from buildings near the beach and the brighter light of sky glow cause them to go in the wrong direction. They make their way toward the artificial light instead of toward water. These young turtles are more likely to be eaten by birds, crabs, and other predators. They may fall into chlorinated swimming pools, be struck by vehicles, or walk into bonfires.

Leatherback sea turtles emerging from nest.

Lighting on piers or platforms in the water also causes problems for emerging turtles. Hatchlings may walk along the beach toward lights instead of directly entering the water. Those that reach the ocean may be eaten by fish that were also attracted to artificial light.

Hatchlings have only a limited amount of energy to reach the water and migrate to offshore feeding grounds. Turtles that become exhausted trying to find the sea are more likely to be killed by predators. Those that do not reach the water before the sun rises will dry out and die. Even if they arrive at the ocean safely, only one hatchling in every thousand will reach adulthood.

HELPING SEA TURTLES

Scientists are trying to find ways to help sea turtles. On some beaches, they set up wire-mesh cages to protect turtle nests. The cages stop skunks, raccoons, foxes, armadillos, and other predators from eating the eggs. The hatchlings are captured after they emerge and released at a dark beach.

Unfortunately, the cages are not very effective. Turtles still waste their energy crawling inside the cages. Self-releasing cages were tried at darker beaches, but low levels of light still led hatchlings to walk in the wrong direction.

Scientists have also tried digging up turtle eggs and bringing them to hatcheries. Some hatcheries were fenced to keep turtles in and predators out. The scientists reburied the eggs in holes meant to imitate natural nests. When the eggs hatched, staff collected young turtles and released them at dark beaches. The newborns had to find their own way to the water.

This is an expensive solution and one that does not solve the real problem of light pollution. Saving turtles with hatcheries and cages has not been very successful.

TURTLE-FRIENDLY LIGHTING

Small turtle populations are as important as large ones. They help ensure genetic diversity within the species. For this reason, light pollution needs to be eliminated on all beaches used by nesting turtles. Hatchlings that emerge from nests farther from lights are more likely to be successful. Even a decrease in lighting will help.

People visiting or living in coastal areas can help reduce light pollution by turning off lights that can be seen from beaches. Residents can make a difference by installing fewer lights and choosing not to use decorative lighting. Windows that face the ocean can be tinted or covered with window films, blinds, or dark curtains. Using bulbs with lower wattages and moving lamps away from windows reduces the amount of light escaping into the night sky. Residents can also help by blocking reflective surfaces that shine light onto beaches. Natural shields, such as vegetation, are ideal.

When lights are necessary, building owners can use turtle-friendly lighting. Red or amber, low-pressure, sodium-vapor bulbs and shielded lights that direct light down to the ground are good choices. Short fixtures that concentrate light where it is needed are wise, too. Timers and motion sensors can help ensure lights are only on when essential. In some coastal areas around the world, people recognize how light pollution affects sea turtles. They have rules to make sure property owners turn off outdoor lights during nesting season. This is an important step to take, but difficult to enforce. Because sky glow is also a problem for turtles, responsible lighting needs to occur both inland and on the coast.

PROTECT TURTLES

In Volusia County, Florida, people who fail to protect sea turtles from harmful lighting can be fined. They are charged up to $1,000 the first time a lighting law is broken and up to $5,000 per day after that. Offenders can also be charged a one-time $15,000 fine. They face even more legal problems if their lighting causes a sea turtle injury or death.

COMMUNITY NEWS

Birds and Light

I like to read so much I'll read almost anything. Every day, the paperboy delivers the *Edmonton Journal*. I always check out the comics page, the horoscopes (even though I don't believe them), and Ann Landers' advice column. She answers people who write in with their problems. I don't know what she's talking about half the time, but I like to see the funny way people sign their names—*Mad in Montana, Frustrated in Farmington, Determined in Delaware,* and that kind of thing.

One Tuesday there's something new in the paper. It's a page with puzzles, pen pal lists, and stories. It's a club just for kids. I send in my name and address and the newspaper sends me a badge that says: *Cub Reporter*. One day, the kids' page advertises a writing contest. I make up a poem about birds and mail it in. Six weeks later, the winners are announced. I don't win but something good still happens. My name is in the paper! Next to my name it says: *Honorable Mention*.

The way I see it, they liked my poem but ran out of prizes. Because my name is in the paper, something else good happens! The editor of the *Sherwood Park Star* sends me a letter in the mail. The letter says:

Dear Joan,

Congratulations on receiving an honorable mention in the Edmonton Journal Writing contest. I see you are a writer and you live in Sherwood Park. Would you like to write for the Sherwood Park Star? We will pay you 10 cents per column inch. If this interests you, please mail your articles to the address on this letter. Measure the length of your article after you see it in the paper and let us know how much we owe you when you send in your next submission.

I look forward to hearing from you.

Sincerely, Editor, Sherwood Park Star

Wow! Last week I was delivering the local newspaper. Now I've got a job writing for it! The editor may know I'm only twelve, but the readers won't. I'm not going to tell them.

The first story I write is about the tree swallows in our backyard. Every time I go near the birdhouse, the parent birds dive bomb my head. Most of the time, I'm careful not to get too close to the swallow nest. I don't want the birds to abandon their eggs. But one day I hear "cheep, cheep, cheep." I drag the stepladder up to the birdhouse and peek inside. The baby birds have gigantic mouths that look like they're pulled down in a frown. I think the babies are happy but I know Mama and Papa are mad! They swoop and soar around me. I hop down the ladder and drag it away.

My tree swallow story is in the paper the following week. I measure it with a ruler and carefully note it is 9.5 inches long. I will earn ninety-five cents. That's almost enough to buy five chocolate bars. I decide to start writing really long sentences so I'll earn more, but I soon discover long sentences look ridiculous in a newspaper column.

It's time to write my second article but I don't have any ideas! What will I do? I've been discovered and become a has-been, all in the same month. Maybe I should write to Ann Landers about my problem. As soon as I think about the advice lady, I know what to do! I'll ask people to send me questions about birds. If someone asks me something I can't answer, I'll go the library. I can look up what I need to know, then write the answer in my own words.

To get started, I make up questions. This is fun! The best part is making up names of people to ask the questions. I

Light pours out of what must be a zillion windows. It's midnight!

Light pollution from skyscrapers and other sources may affect these tree swallows when it's time to migrate south.

use the names of every member of my family, including pets. BPG (my budgie—Blue Pepper Galat) wants to know: *How long do birds live?* Puzzled in the Park asks: *How do migrating birds find their way?* Midnight Mama wonders: *Why do birds migrate at all?*

The newspaper editor likes my question-and-answer bird column idea. I'm so glad! It's fun making up the questions and finding out the answers. Once in a while, I even get mail from real people with real questions. Sometimes people who read the column bring me injured birds to care for and release. I get a sparrow named Fred, a seagull named Jonathon, and a magpie called Mason.

Just to be safe, I always write each bird column two weeks before it's due. I'm worried if I don't do it early I'll end up in a last minute panic, not have all the facts I need, and lose my job.

One day I get a surprise that means I better get even further ahead. Dad has a plan to take me with him on a ten-day trip to New York City. He grew up in Brooklyn and some of the family still lives there. I'm so excited I have a million questions. Can we go to Nathan's for hotdogs? What about the Statue of Liberty and Coney Island? I haven't been to New York since we lived three hours away—in Maryland, near Washington, D.C.

A month later, Dad and I board a Northwest Airlines flight to Minneapolis. We change planes and after too many hours of me trying to sit still, the pilot finally makes the announcement I've been dying to hear. "Fasten your seatbelt for landing."

I peer through my oval window and see the sprawling glow of New York. The plane drops lower and more skyscrapers appear than I can count. This is not like Edmonton at all. Light pours out of what must be a zillion windows. It's midnight! Are people actually inside there working?

The city goes on and on and on. I can't believe how long it takes to fly over the endless stream of lit-up buildings, streets, and cars. The plane circles lower as we approach La Guardia Airport and I see a bridge. Its cables are lit with lights that swoop in elegant curves between each tower.

Dad peers out the window and tells me it's the Brooklyn Bridge. Finally we land, get our luggage, and find Aunts Rose and Florence, who have come to pick us up. They drive us to their house and show me the bedroom where I'm to sleep. I'm tired but my eyes won't stay closed. Lights from the street shine into my room, and the sound of fire and police sirens seems to go on all night.

After a couple of days hanging out at the house, I'm so bored I refold every item of clothing in my suitcase. I want to go to Owl's Head Park. It's only a block away on the Hudson River but the answer is "No." I'm not allowed to go there alone. Nor am I allowed to walk to the corner store by myself. I'm not even allowed to sit on the front steps alone. If it's so unsafe, how did Dad manage to grow up here?

Finally, relief! We take the subway to Manhattan to see the tallest buildings in New York—the World Trade Center. The elevator zooms us up 100 floors, making my stomach feel like it isn't travelling as fast as the rest of my body. We arrive at the Observation Deck and step outside to see the view of Manhattan, Brooklyn, New Jersey, and the harbor. We're so high up we look down at the Empire State Building, once the world's tallest structure.

I'm thinking this is a lot more fun than hanging around the house, when I spot something moving. Turning toward the motion, I see a bird on the flat roof, on the other side of the safety barrier. It's trying to fly but can only stretch out one wing and flutter sideways. The bird has a red forehead and throat, a strong, straight beak, black and white wings, and yellow underparts. I recognize this species because it lives in Alberta, too. It's a yellow-bellied sapsucker.

Dad comes over to see what I'm looking at and we wonder what a woodpecker is doing up here and how it got injured. Could it have hit one of the glass windows and fallen here? I want to help it but what can I do? It's close to the place where the building drops off, 100 stories to the ground.

I ask Dad if we should tell someone, but he doesn't think anyone is going to risk his life to save a bird that might not live anyway. I try to change his mind but he insists, and

then it's time to go. Looking back as we line up for the elevator, I feel as helpless as the woodpecker that can't fly.

MIGRATING IN THE DARK

Northern regions have plenty of bugs and great bird habitat. Many bird species migrate north in the spring to take advantage of all this food and territory. They raise their young and build up fat reserves to help them fly south in the fall. As summer ends, days get shorter, air becomes cooler, and food harder to find. Birds know it is time to migrate when day length changes.

Two-thirds of migrating birds fly after sunset. Night travel makes it easier to avoid hawks, eagles, and other predators that hunt in the day. Flying at night is also easier because wind dies down.

Birds have special adaptations that tell them which way to go. They look at the positions of the stars and Sun. They watch the landscape. They sense the location of the Earth's magnetic field and use it like a compass.

Birds have trouble seeing the stars when light pollution is present. The light makes them disoriented—mixed up about which way they should go. When artificial light or cloudy skies make stars hard to see, migrating birds depend on the Earth's magnetic field. Unfortunately, artificial light may also interfere with the internal magnetic compass birds rely upon. On dark nights, artificial light can cause birds to leave their flight paths. They may never reach their destinations.

Young birds with little or no migrating experience are most confused by lights. Some stare into light until they fly into it and strike a structure. They may die on impact or knock themselves out and fall to the ground. Many die or starve because they are too injured to find food.

Birds that survive the fall are often too tired to escape predators. Even birds that are unhurt may not survive migration. Artificial light can cause them to waste the fat reserves they built up for their long trip. Even in the normal course of their lives—apart from

STAY AWAY!

High towers are built to transmit radio, telephone, and mobile phone signals. Bright lights on these towers warn pilots: "Stay away!" But nocturnal birds don't know they need to stay away, too. They are attracted to the light. Millions of migrating birds have flown into towers and died.

times they migrate—birds circle areas that are brightly lit because they do not want to fly back into the dark.

Aimless flying is an unnatural behavior that can limit how long birds will live. Birds need to spend their time and energy on survival—finding food, mating, nest building, caring for young, and migrating.

BABYSITTING ROBINS

Early one morning, Mom calls me to the phone. I'm kind of dopey in the morning because I like to stay up late and look at the stars. A lady who reads my newspaper column must have looked our last name up in the phone book. She asks me if I can come over and birdsit the young robins in her spruce tree. The babies keep falling out of the nest. The lady puts them back in and they fall back out. She's worried a cat will get them if no one is there to save them.

I cover the mouthpiece to ask Mom and she takes the phone from me. She finds out the lady is our neighbor's sister. Mom decides I can go, so I ride my bike over to babysit the robins while the lady runs her errands.

When I arrive, the lady says I can call her Andrea. I feel so grown up calling an adult by her first name. Andrea says she won't be gone very long because she's so tired. The robin's singing woke her up when it was still dark, calling a steady, "cheerily, cheerily–cheer-up, cheer-up, cheer-up." I know robins like to sing at dawn but they aren't nocturnal birds.

Why would a robin sing at night? Before I can think too much about it, Andrea waves goodbye and it's just the early birds and me.

I sit on the front steps in a lawn chair and read my library book. Every four pages, I check the ground beneath the tree. All is well. The babies are staying where they belong. But after my twelfth page, I see a robin the size of a small potato hopping across the roots that weave in and out of the ground beneath the tree. Setting my book on the chair, I rise in slow motion and scan for evil cats.

"Hi, baby robin. Don't panic. I'm just going to slowly walk over, pick you up, and put you back with your brothers and sisters." I bend down and cup my hands around the robin. His chest is a mottled blend of black, white, and red. Tufts of wispy feathers stick out at funny angles and his yellow beak looks too big for his body. I've never held such a small bird before. He's as light as a handful of cotton balls but his claws feel firm against my skin. The robin scrambles against my palm for balance but doesn't seem to mind being held.

I wonder how many times the lady has already saved this robin.

A ladder is pushed snug against the tree. I cradle the warm bird against my stomach with one hand and climb the ladder, holding on with the other. Dad would not like to see me climbing a ladder this way. Mom would not like to see me climb one at all. I set the robin back into the nest. Three others crowd the space but he wiggles his way in. With both hands free, I scoot down the ladder and back to my book. I'm glad the mother robin didn't show up and swoop at me.

Years later, I get a job writing information to go with the displays at Edmonton's nature center. I learn that baby robins live on the ground after they outgrow the nest. It seems my babysitting services weren't needed. Still, I'm glad to have met someone else who likes birds enough to get a sitter for them, even if one did keep her up with its odd nighttime singing.

EARLY BIRDS

People often find they have more energy at certain times. They may call themselves "early birds" or "night owls." Birds and other animals are the same but they don't just *like* day or night the best; they *need* to be active at these times in order to survive.

Most songbirds are diurnal. That means they are adapted to use energy in the day and rest at night. They seek food, build nests, and care for their young in the daytime. Robins are songbirds that begin and end each day in song. They sing to warn other birds to stay away from their territory.

When light pollution is present, robins sing earlier in the morning and later at night. They may even sing all night! Light pollution may cause some bird species to breed too early in the spring. This is a problem if the food they need is not yet plentiful. Artificial light can also cause breeding seasons to last longer than normal. Food sources may become scarce and weather harsher.

School's Out

In Alberta, school closes near the end of June. Every year we celebrate with a wiener roast at the acreage. The acreage is a three-and-a-half-acre piece of land my parents bought just four miles from Sherwood Park. Dad calls it "Tara" after the name of a plantation in some book called *Gone with the Wind*. They say they might build a house there one day. I sure hope so, even though I'd have to take a bus to school instead of walking like I do now.

I love going to the acreage. Part of it is a field but most of it is aspen forest. Red squirrels chatter above the trails that wind through the woods. The best part is the pond. I've spotted Canada geese, mallard ducks, and beaver in the water. I can tell where the porcupines have been. They always leave stripped tree branches along the path that leads to the clearing near the pond. We follow this trail to the picnic table and fire pit.

I always build the fire. It must be laid so well that a single match can ignite it. This is a family tradition. Using more than one match results in teasing. I gather dry grass, leaves, and small sticks into a pile, then make a teepee around the kindling with longer sticks I find on the ground. Good thing it hasn't rained lately. The wood is nice and dry. Dad hacks at some logs with a hatchet and piles the pieces nearby. I'll add them as the fire catches.

"Ready?" I ask. Mom and Dad gather around the fire pit for the big moment. I strike a white-tipped wooden match against a rock, catch a whiff of sulfur, and hold the flame to the bottom of my pile.

The grass turns into carrot-colored lines that ignite the leaves. Orange flames flicker and thick gray smoke pours through the top. Sparks crackle and fly through the air like fireflies. Suddenly the blaze stops. I crouch low, tuck a wayward strand of hair behind one ear, and blow on the fragile cinders. The flames rise up once more, and this time one of the larger sticks ignites. I run to the spot where Dad chops logs, gather a handful of wood chips, then dash back and feed the flames one chip at a time. The fire takes.

"That was close," says Dad.

"Not close at all!" I insist. We grin and Mom hands us our wiener forks.

Long after the food is put away, we sit around the fire. I poke at the coals with a long stick. Summer days in Alberta are long. It's cloudy tonight so it gets dark a bit earlier. But we still see light. It comes from the fireflies flashing their green-yellow lights on the other side of the pond.

FIREFLIES

Also called lightning bugs, fireflies are members of the beetle family. Adult fireflies are important flower pollinators. A chemical reaction in their abdomens creates light in an area of their bodies called "the lantern." Dark nights allow them to use light to communicate with each other. Their flashing patterns of light attract mates, defend territory, or warn predators away. The flickers might mean "Come here," "Watch out," or "Go away!"

Fireflies are attracted to artificial light. Those that gather near lights are more likely to be eaten by frogs, spiders, bats, birds, and other fireflies. Artificial lights blind and distract fireflies, as well as interfere with mating and hunting.

In some firefly species, all males in an area may flash their lights at the exact same time. This is called synchronous flashing. Scientists think males may attract more females this way. But species trying to flash together lose their

NIGHT TOURISTS

Campfires, outdoor laser shows, and even fireworks cause light pollution. Fortunately, there are other ways to enjoy the night without disturbing the environment. In some places, travelers take tours to see fireflies flash their light. Parks and nature centers may offer nighttime hikes to spot owls. Public observatories welcome visitors to look at stars, planets, and other night sky objects through their telescopes. Astronomy clubs may even host star parties for viewing the night sky at a dark location. Sometimes they're held during meteor showers.

Flying at night protects this long-eared bat's thin wings from daytime heat.

ECOSYSTEMS

In nature, organisms have relatio-ships with one another. This community of relationships is called an ecosystem. An ecosystem might exist in a puddle or include an entire forest. If light pollution causes one species to disappear from a habitat, other parts of the ecosystem suffer. Light can upset the entire ecosystem if it causes a species to become extinct or allows a new species to take over.

rhythm after a car with headlights goes by. Even a flashlight can interrupt fireflies' rhythm.

The magic of the warm summer evenings would be lost if fireflies became extinct. Scientists believe light pollution is one of the reasons North America's firefly populations have shrunk.

ANIMALS NEED DARKNESS

I'm sure it's easier to be a human than to be an animal. At bedtime, I shut the blinds, close the curtains, and crawl into bed. Everyone knows it's easier to fall asleep in the dark. I once saw Aunt Florence sleep wearing an eye mask to keep the light out. It must have worked because she was snoring pretty loudly.

A lot of animals need dark to sleep, too. Sleep is necessary for survival. It keeps the mind and body working properly.

Animals that don't get enough shut-eye become forgetful.

Nocturnal animals, like bats, are active at night and sleep during the day. Other species are diurnal—adapted to be active during the day and sleep at night. Some animals, like porcupines, are crepuscular. That means that they are most active during the dimly lit twilight hours around sunrise and sunset.

No matter what time they are most active, all animals need darkness. Nocturnal animals are adapted to capture food and avoid enemies in dark environments. Animals that are active at night face less competition for food, water, shelter, and space. Diurnal animals, like red squirrels, need darkness to hide from predators and feel safe enough to sleep. But squirrels can't close drapes or put on an eye mask like Aunt Flo.

Sleeping Under the Stars

A few days after our campfire at the acreage, my friend Denise comes for a sleepover. The thermometer reaches thirty degrees and the air in the house feels like it's coming out of a popcorn popper. We decide to sleep in the back yard under the stars.

Even on hot days, Alberta nights get cool. After supper we haul every sleeping bag we can find onto the backyard lawn. It takes nearly an hour to blow up the air mattresses, lay out the bedding, and find batteries to fit Dad's flashlights.

The Sun doesn't set until close to 10:00 PM this time of year, and the light lingers orange in the western sky a long time after that. Even if it was dark we wouldn't feel like sleeping, but close to midnight Mom insists we be quiet. We get into our pajamas, climb into our sleeping bags, and giggle about almost everything we say. As it gets darker, the plaid pattern on my sleeping bag fades to black. We turn on the flashlights and make designs against the wall of the house, taking turns trying to guess what the other draws with the light beam.

I wave the flashlight in slow motion, trying to outline a house—a square with a triangle on top—when something hard zings into my hand. I scream and drop the light and fight the tangle of blankets to get up. Denise doesn't know what's going on but shoots out of bed, too.

"Something hit my hand!" I shout.

"What, what?" she bellows back. A light goes on in the neighbor's house and we turn our hollers to hisses. She points her light at the ground where my flashlight fell and we see a dull brown bug crawl across the lens. It's the size of an eraser and kind of beetle-shaped.

When I lean down for a better look, another one lands on the light. I kick the flashlight with my foot, then reach down and turn it off. She turns her light off, too. My heart pounds and neither of us wants to get back into bed.

Deciding to go for a walk around the block, we slip flip-flops on our feet and robes over our PJ's. I peer into the dining room window to make sure Dad isn't still up watching TV. All is quiet. We tiptoe around the front and walk down the block, whispering jokes about how we'll claim to be sleepwalking if my parents happen to look out the window. No one else is walking or in their yards, or even driving by. The night feels friendly until we notice more of the giant bugs, along with dozens of moths, under the streetlights. I start watching for them but my heart no longer pounds in horror. I only mind bugs when they surprise me.

We round the last corner toward home and I see something more important to worry about. A car with its headlights on is parked in front of our house and I know it wasn't there before. I whisper to Denise and we slow our steps and watch as the driver leans over to kiss the passenger. Suddenly I realize it's my sister and her date and his window is halfway down.

I use my softest voice to tell Denise, but when our eyes meet laughter bubbles up our throats and out our mouths. She snorts and I cover my mouth with my hand and start to run. Denise sprints alongside me. Suddenly the toe of my flip-flop bends the wrong way and I fly headfirst onto the lawn by the car. She flies past me as I scramble up and follow her around the house.

About two billion insects exist for every human being on Earth!

We dive back into our sleeping bags and lie as still as we can, though the inside of my chest feels like horse hooves racing around a track. Will they come after us? Will my sister tell my parents tomorrow? It's quiet for the longest time and I hear Denise's even breaths. She's asleep. I stare at the light and dark patterns on the Moon, tilting my head one way to find the rabbit and the other way to see the face of the man on the Moon, until my blinks last longer and longer and I fall asleep.

BIODIVERSITY MATTERS

"Bug! Snake! Bat! Spider!" Shout one of these words and see what happens. One person might panic while another barely reacts. Would it really matter if certain creatures disappeared? The answer is "Yes!" A healthy environment needs biodiversity—a variety of species of plants and animals.

Biodiversity is important because all organisms in a habitat contribute to a healthy ecosystem. The animals and plants in an ecosystem do not just live near each other. They depend on one another to survive. Birds, insects, and bats pollinate plants. Bees depend on plant pollen to make honey. Animals help spread plant seeds. Birds, bats, spiders, fish, reptiles, and many other hungry predators need insects for food.

Plants and animals are adapted to interact with one another under natural conditions. Each organism needs to find food, territory, and a mate, but only a limited supply exists. When one species is more successful at getting what it needs, it outcompetes other species. Unnatural light can impact an entire ecosystem's health when it causes animals to change their natural behaviors. Some change by moving toward light. Others avoid lit habitat.

Artificial light at night upsets the way predators and prey compete with one another. It makes it harder for predators like

Insects attracted to streetlamp.

owls to hunt mice and other small creatures. Light allows prey to see owls coming and escape. Lizards attracted to insects at lights may forage outside their natural habitat and become more successful at capturing food than those that avoid light. The light-lovers out-compete the dark-lovers, creating an imbalance between species in the ecosystem.

Lights can also impact reproductive behavior. Certain insects and frogs only mate when night is at its darkest. Their breeding habits depend on natural lighting conditions. Lower insect populations can lead to smaller animal populations. Animals that cannot find food may leave, die, or even become extinct within a local area.

When one species disappears, others are impacted. Take away bats and there may be too many mosquitoes. Take away ladybugs and there may be too many aphids. Take away coyotes and there may be more rabbits than an area can support.

INSECTS AND LIGHT

Even a little bit of light will interfere with the natural behavior of nocturnal insects. When light pollution is present, these species become less active to avoid their enemies.

Artificial light forms a barrier to insect movement and migration. Some species won't cross roads lit by streetlights. This line of light is called the "crash barrier." It may stop insects from traveling in the direction they need to go. Light can cause migrating species to become disoriented and lose their way. Insects unable to migrate are likely to die.

As cities and towns build more houses and erect more lights, habitat becomes lost or fragmented—broken into smaller areas. The lights attract insects away from natural habitat. Fewer insects live in areas with light pollution. Fewer insects mean fewer plant and animal species.

INSECTS NEED THE MOON

Scientists believe insects use the Moon to help them find their way. They use the Moon as a guide to fly in a straight line. But things go wrong when insects mistake artificial light for moonlight. They try to maintain their angle to the light instead of to the Moon. This makes them fly in circles around the light. They may think they have actually reached the Moon!

Insects may circle until they fall to the ground in exhaustion. The light stops them from doing what they need to do to survive— capture food, avoid predators, and breed. Insects that fixate on a light may fly into it and die from the impact or from touching the hot bulb. Those that land safely are still easy prey for bats, birds, spiders, and insect predators.

Insects will fly to lights as far as 400 feet (120 meters) away. Lights that draw insects away from their habitat and kill them create a "vacuum cleaner effect." It's as if all the insects have been sucked out of an area.

Lights can cause entire insect populations to shrink. These deaths hurt the food chain. Frogs, salamanders, bats, birds, and small mammals are the first to be impacted by low insect populations.

Some insects take advantage of light and are active for longer periods than normal. Light may allow them to prey on other species more successfully. Light-loving species may find it easier to out-compete other insects. Unfortunately, their longer-than-normal active period upsets the ecosystem's natural balance.

MOTHS NEED NIGHT

Almost all of the world's 150,000 moth species are nocturnal. Even though they need darkness to eat and reproduce, most species are attracted to light. Artificial light may lead them to places with unusable habitat like rocky islands or oil platforms.

Most moth species feed on the nectar of white or yellow night-blooming flowers. These colors are easiest for moths to see in dim light. Unfortunately, artificial light makes it hard to spot food.

Moths depend on camouflage for protection. Their coloring hides them when conditions are natural but not when artificial light is present. Moths near lights are easy for birds and bats to see and catch.

Going from dark to bright light causes moths to become temporarily blind. This condition lasts longer for moths than it does for humans. Moths may try to prevent vision loss by staying in lit areas, but even those that do leave will probably return. Moths' memories are not long enough to remember why they left the light in the first place!

ESCAPE
At night, disturbed moths avoid danger by flying upward— toward starlight or moonlight. They may react to artificial light as if it is an escape route.

To the Coast—
Artificial Light & Frogs

I heave my tan Samsonite suitcase into the trunk of the Pumpkin. We're driving to Vancouver Island, in British Columbia, for a summer holiday. As usual, my sisters stay home. As we wave goodbye, Mom calls to them out the window, "No parties!"

It's a thirteen-hour drive to the ferry terminal. It will take another hour and a half to reach the island. The entire trip will take us from the fields and woodlands around home, through the foothills, then to the Rocky Mountains. I guess I won't be stargazing from the car on this trip. Mom insists we travel in the daytime. She's worried we'll hit an animal if we drive at night.

Elk, moose, deer, and great-horned rams often cross mountain roads. Animals blinded by headlights can be injured or killed by cars. Trains on the railway tracks hit them, too. It's

dangerous for both animals and people. Even at home, we see porcupine, deer, skunk, and sometimes cats or dogs that have been hit by cars. They're easy to spot if you look for ravens and crows—always the first to find roadkill.

When we stop for a picnic supper, I go for a walk and spot a roundish lump of something on the side of the road. Up close, I realize it is a dead porcupine—back end squished, a splotch of red-black blood drying on the sandy gravel, and quills scattered like toothpicks at odd angles in the grass bordering the ditch. Except for the back end, which is pretty gross, the porcupine looks like it's sleeping. I feel bad for it and wonder why it had to be on the road just when a car came by. But I'm also glad about something else. There's just enough breeze to save me from smelling it.

Using my nails so I don't get poked, I pick up as many quills as I can find. Each one is thinner than a piece of raw spaghetti, white tapering to a black point, and hollow. I'm wondering if I can find a way to prop them upright on my sisters' kitchen chairs when we're back home when another idea pops into my head. Setting the quills in a little pile on the road's shoulder, I head back to our picnic spot, ducking low behind some bushes once I'm close.

Mom is making sandwiches. Dad is squirting water onto the Pumpkin's windshield from the ancient bottle he keeps in the trunk. He circles the car and rubs the glass with a rag as I try to sidle up to the trash bin. Success! I grab the white plastic bag Mom tossed earlier and sprint back to the ditch.

Using the bag like a glove so I don't have to touch the porcupine, I grab a leg and try to lift it up. Uh-oh. This animal is heavier than it looks—definitely more than a twenty-pound bag of potatoes. It falls to the ground with a thud, and I discover the furry leg I thought I was holding is actually a quill-covered leg. I'm stabbed—right through the bag.

Lucky for me, the quill does not go deep. I pull it out, suck on my bleeding finger, and try to figure out whether I should try to drag it to our picnic site or just give up. Mom calls me for lunch and suddenly I know just what to do. I stuff the bag in my pocket, crouch down by the porcupine and call, "Come here for a sec. I found something!"

Roadkill, including porcupine, racoon and deer, are all too common scenes along our roads.

Mom and Dad follow my voice to the road. When they're in sight, I pretend to pet the porcupine but really just glide my hand through the air overtop its back. "Look at my friend," I call. They're too far to see my friend is dead. Dad runs up, grabs my hand, and pulls me back from the porcupine. I crack up laughing so hard I have to cross my legs. They put on stern faces and we have a talk about rabies and fleas but, in the end, Dad just shakes his head and Mom presses her lips together, thinking I can't tell she's hiding a smile.

EYES COLLECT LIGHT

Light pollution makes it harder for animals with dark-adapted eyes to find food, hide from predators, locate mates, and avoid danger. Even small amounts of light may cause problems for nocturnal species.

Vision is the most important sense for many animals. The retina in the eye contains photoreceptors made up of rod and cone cells. These cells collect the light the eye needs to see. Animals with lots of cone cells have good color vision and see greater detail—like gravel on the road or insects on a leaf. Species with good color vision are less likely to see well at night.

Animals with a lot of rod cells cannot see color or detail very well. They see better in dim light or when it is completely dark. Rod cells enable owls to see mice more than a football field away—as long as it's dark!

Certain mammals, like deer and raccoons, have a secret weapon—the *tapetum lucidum*. Located behind the retina, this part of the eye reflects light the rod and cone cells did not capture. It improves night vision by doubling how much light the eyes can use. If you ever notice an animal caught in light at night, you'll see its eyes appear to glow. This happens when light strikes the tapetum lucidum.

GOODBYE HABITAT

As we drive, I lean my head against the car window and stare at the trees whizzing past. Every time I sit this way, the same picture enters my brain. An imaginary invisible pole

Imagine what it's like to see without good color vision. Next time you're outside in the dark, see how well you can make out colors. You might be surprised to find out humans are color-blind in dim light.

extends from the car and slices through the trees. Each falls, one at a time, in a graceful curve, then disappears.

Suddenly the trees really are gone and not just because it's getting dark. I stare at a field that's bare except for a half-dozen mounds of trunks and leafless branches pushed into piles. Scraggly roots, looking like broken witch brooms, dangle uselessly in the air. Smoke smolders upward from one clump, and a cloud of dust rises up behind a farmer's tractor as he pushes more debris into a pile.

The only natural area left is a small circle of shrubs around a pond. The stubble of a crop, probably wheat or barley, is shorn in a tight path along the water's edge. It must have been planted as close to the water as a tractor could get without sinking. I wonder if the farmer plans to drain the pond and farm that land, too. I wonder what will become of the wildlife.

My body lurches forward as Dad stops the car. Peering over the front seat, I see a monstrous yellow digging machine with claws

that hack at the ditch. Two massive lights mounted on skeletal steel frames cast glaring beams across the ground. A man in orange coveralls holds up a stop sign and we wait.

Mom sighs, resigned to still being on the road at night. I roll down my window a few inches and the smell of hot tar seeps in. Dad says something but I'm not listening; I hear the chirp of boreal chorus frogs. Their call is like the sound your thumb makes if you pull it across the teeth of a plastic comb—but more musical.

I've always loved the sound of frogs but I've never wanted to hold one. It might jump onto my arm or, worse, down my shirt. I know from my newspaper column research that waterbirds eat frogs and frogs eat a ton of insects. The only bad thing about them is when one of my sisters catches a frog and chases me, shrieking, "Kiss the frog and meet the handsome prince." I guess that's an annoying thing about my sisters, not the frogs.

Dad slaps at a mosquito and twists around to wave a hand near my face. "Roll up the window." I crank it up and turn my eyes back to the guy on the tractor just as he flicks on his headlights. The sudden brightness makes me blink and turn away. When we start moving again and I glance back, the tractor is spinning around, its lights shining through the dust and onto the soil.

ARTIFICIAL LIGHT AND AMPHIBIANS

Amphibians include frogs, toads, and salamanders—important members of the food chain. They eat amazing numbers of insects, invertebrates, and vertebrates. They also serve as prey for many predators.

Light pollution reduces how much usable habitat is available to amphibians. Habitat loss results in fewer species of frogs and toads, as well as smaller populations.

Nocturnal frogs and toads are some of the first species to suffer when light pollution makes habitat less desirable.

After wetland loss, light pollution is the biggest cause of amphibian death. Light that disrupts night vision leaves amphibians unable to recognize possible mates. They need darkness to breed and avoid predators, but darkness does not always arrive.

FROGS AND LIGHT

Many frog species gather under streetlights. Scientists are not sure whether frogs like light or whether they only come to feed on easy-to-capture insects. Frogs that leave natural habitat to go toward light are more likely to be caught by predators. Others are hit by cars when they cross roads to reach lights.

Artificial light creates other problems for frogs. Light that shines for even a minute during the night can interfere with melatonin production. Melatonin controls frogs' ability to change their color. They change colors to help them adjust to different temperatures, blend in with their surroundings, or discourage predators.

Shy Brazilian tree frog at night.

I CAN'T GROW UP!

Frogs lay clumps of eggs in ponds or pools of water that dry up when spring turns to summer. Tadpoles live in the water until they grow hind legs, forelegs, and lungs. Now the tadpoles are frogs and can live on land. But some tadpoles do not grow up. Fewer tadpoles turn into frogs when artificial light shines at night. Tadpoles born in temporary pools of water die when they cannot hop away before the water dries up in spring.

I WON'T SING!

Male frogs are the only ones who sing. They call out to attract females. Different species make different sounds from croaks and chirps to whistles. Scientists discovered male green frogs are less vocal when artificial light is present. Quieter frogs mean fewer frogs, since females select mates when they hear males sing. A little light may cause a lot of problems if light prevents males from attracting females.

I CAN'T SEE!

Have you ever noticed what happens when you go from a super dark area to an extremely bright place? It is very hard to see. After a few minutes, your eyes recover and the temporary blindness is gone. The same thing happens to amphibians, but their vision does not return as quickly.

Light levels that change suddenly at night can make a frog hopping mad. Imagine a frog foraging for food in a ditch by a highway. There are no lights along the road. The frog's eyes are used to the dark. He can see the prey he wants to eat. Suddenly a car approaches. Its headlights shine into the ditch and the frog's eyes. Light causes a chemical reaction in the frog's eyes. The frog is temporarily blinded. It cannot see anything.

The frog will not see until its eyes get used to the dark again. Recovery time depends on how dark-adapted the frog's eyes had become. It can take hours if the light was very bright and other light pollution is present.

Habitats with areas of extreme light and areas of extreme dark are also a problem. Picture a lawn where ground lights make distinct patches of light next to patches of darkness. A frog traveling a short distance hops across ground with vastly different light levels. Every time it enters a dark area, the frog has to wait for its eyes to adapt. Frogs exposed to changing light conditions find it more difficult to capture fast-moving, camouflaged prey.

Shearwaters at sea.

Ocean Lights

It feels like I have lived through the longest day of my life when we finally reach the ferry terminal well after supper. The boat is as long as two football fields. Mom says 470 vehicles can fit inside. Dad drives the Pumpkin onto the ramp and follows a station wagon into the belly of the boat.

It's dark. I feel the rumble of the engine, smell diesel fumes, and wonder how far below the water we are. A shiver runs down my spine. After Dad parks, we get the binoculars from the trunk and climb metal steps up and up and up until we finally reach the viewing deck. Light from the sinking sun hits my face and the shiver is gone.

The greenish-gray water in the Strait of Georgia separates Vancouver Island from the mainland. This part of the Pacific Ocean looks calm. I won't see great crashing waves until we go beachcombing.

I scan the water with my binoculars. It's hard to hold them steady so I prop my elbows against the rail. I'm rewarded with the sudden appearance of a great blue heron. Its giant rounded wings and neck folded back against the body make it easy to identify. I spot double-crested cormorants, brown pelicans, and lots of sooty shearwaters. They're about the size of a gull and rather plain with their dark gray feathers, but I'm excited to see them because they're near-threatened in some places.

Every time I see a new species, I pull a piece of paper out of my pocket and write it down. I'm making a list of every bird I've ever seen. Most of the species on my list are from the aspen woodlands and grasslands around home. I don't have any seabirds, unless you count seagulls.

I watch birds until the Sun sets behind the island. As the sky turns from blue to black, a light forms a long dark shadow of me. It stretches out from my sneakers. I notice that lights on the island outline the shore, roads, and harbor. I see lights on the pier, on boats crossing the water, and on a cruise ship. I feel cheated of the night.

We go inside to the restaurant and get some hotdogs. A great blob of yellow mustard plops onto my shorts. I have an inability to eat mustard without getting it on my clothes. We sit for a bit, then walk back out onto the deck. I'm surprised to see so many seabirds circling the ferry. There's no time to try to identify them. A horn sounds and we see Vancouver Island ahead. It's time to get back into the car. A bright light marks the staircase we need. Fluttering moths surround the light fixture. One smacks into the bulb and fries. Sizzle. My nose wrinkles. Insects aren't my favorite creatures but I still feel sorry for them. Dumb light.

MARINE BIRDS

Artificial lights in ocean environments attract birds from large areas. Some die after swallowing baited hooks near lit boats. Birds may circle lights for hours or days. Others run out of energy and fall into the water. Many seabirds need to flap a long way or take off from a steep cliff before they can fly upward. Birds that fall to the ground may not survive if they cannot get back into the air.

Light reduces the amount of habitat where seabirds can live and raise their young. Intense light pollution causes some species to lay fewer eggs and abandon nests more often. Artificial lighting is a serious problem for threatened and endangered species.

Offshore glare from lights can make it hard for sailors to see markers that show the safest route through shallow and rocky waters.

SHEARWATERS AND PETRELS

Shearwaters and petrels are birds that depend on darkness during the breeding season. Being nocturnal helps protect their young from gulls, raptors, and other day-active predators.

Young birds, called fledglings, look at the patterns of stars in the sky to find their way to water. Fledglings can mistake artificial light with starlight and become confused. When bright lights make the stars and horizon hard to see, birds fly inland instead of toward the sea. These disoriented birds often fly into lit structures.

Young birds are attracted to light for another reason, too. Fledglings eat squid that are bioluminescent—animals that glow with their own light. Young birds that fly toward artificial light expect to find food. Instead they find danger.

OIL PLATFORMS

Oil companies use floating oil rigs to drill for oil under the surface of the ocean. Some rigs are large ships with anchors or propellers to hold them in place. Others rigs are made up of platforms with concrete or steel legs.

People work and live on these platforms, which are kept brightly lit for human safety. Rigs also light up the sky with flare stacks that burn off unneeded gas. Some flares burn up to twenty meters into the air. All this light attracts plankton, fish, birds, and other marine species.

Birds can see flares from long distances. Tens of thousands of birds have been recorded flying into flares. Birds not killed by the fire fall or land in the sea. Any oil in the water will make their feathers less waterproof. Oily feathers can't keep them warm and buoyant. Birds die from exhaustion, starvation, or hypothermia.

TOO MANY
About 6,000 crested auklets once landed on a brightly lit fishing boat near Kodiak Island, Alaska. Together, the birds weighed about 1.5 metric tons. They almost sank the boat!

Oil-drilling platform.

Underwater

I'm dying to swim in the ocean but Dad says there's a rip tide and the water isn't warm enough. We trudge through the deep sand and it trickles through my sandals until we reach the hard-packed shore. I stick my hand in the water but pull it out fast. It's freezing! Maybe Dad knows what he's talking about.

Long Beach on Vancouver Island stretches for ten kilometers, its shore facing the open Pacific. Nothing lies between me and Japan except nearly 8,000 kilometers of saltwater. I stare across the waves and imagine a girl my age in Japan, staring back.

Dad told me people on this beach sometimes find glass floats, lost by people setting fishing nets off the coast of Japan. It would be cool to find a float—I know what to look for because I saw one in a store. It was sea green, the size of a honeydew melon. I scan through the seaweed, driftwood, and muck the waves have rippled up along the shore, but I only spot shells. My toe catches a butter clam with no broken edge. I put it in my pocket and then we make our way back to the Pumpkin for the five-hour drive to Victoria, B.C.'s capital city. I sleep and read and play word games until finally Dad pulls up to Fisherman's Wharf.

The first thing I notice is the fishy smell and my hand zooms up to cover my nose. The second thing I notice is the clutter of boats in the marina—fishing vessels, houseboats, coast guard, water taxis, whale-watching craft, and a sailboat that looks just like the one on the Canadian dime. I can't believe it—there's even a village of floating houses moored to the wharf.

Walking to the Inner Harbour, we spot a boat anchored to the dock with "Underwater

Gardens" lettered across its side. We cross the platform for a closer look and discover it's a floating aquarium. Visitors can go fifteen feet below the water to see a giant octopus, salmon, crabs, and other sea life up close. Mom agrees to go in with me.

Down the steps we climb. The air is cool; it smells like algae, and I can't see very far ahead. The lights down here are dim and I feel closed in. Is this what it's like beneath the ocean?

The first aquarium is labeled *Octopus* but I can't see anything except the sway of seaweed over pebbles. Maybe my eyes need more time to get used to the dark. The next tank is smaller and I notice the profile of a fish, floating in place. Leaning in, I see it's got a bumpy brown head and protruding eye. It's so ugly I pull back and think maybe I don't want to be here after all.

The next display contains a school of iridescent fish with silver-white sides, moving together like dancers in a ballet. A bright light illuminates the water and it

feels more cheerful. I step forward to admire one of the colorful plants. Mom and I put our heads together near the glass, just as it moves and opens its mouth.

Ugh! It must be a sea pen. I don't like animals that look like plants, so I tug Mom's sleeve. "Can we go?" She's already pulling me toward the glowing red exit sign. We climb the stairs and, as the door swings open, bright light surprises me.

MARINE FISH

Fish that live deep underwater are meant to live in a dark environment. Problems occur when people who fish commercially use lights to attract fish and squid to their boats. This light can cause fish to experience eye damage or temporary blindness. Fish that suddenly can't see are more likely to be caught by predators. Artificial light can upset the population balance within an ecosystem if predators become too successful at catching their prey.

FISHING WITH FIRE

Fishing with fire is the oldest way of using light to catch fish. In North America, some Aboriginal people attracted and speared fish by making torches out of stakes that held burning birch bark on one end. Anishinabe used lit birch held in a frame of iron hoops on a pole, about six feet long. One person held the fire over the bow of a canoe, while another speared the fish that came to the light.

Most fish spend time in schools. They swim together in groups that move at the same speed and in the same direction—always with the same species. With so many eyes looking for food, schools locate their meals more easily than a lone fish could. Schooling also protects fish. They watch for danger and swim away from it as a unit. Some predators leave schools alone because they mistake the group for one giant fish.

At sunset, the schools of some species are meant to break up but artificial light can cause fish to remain together for protection. Predatory fish that normally hunt during the day may continue to hunt at night. Light that creates a silhouette around prey allows predators to see them more easily. Fish may capture smaller prey than they would have been able to spot in dark water.

Commercial fishers are another predator looking for schools. It's easier for them to catch fish when so many are close together.

Common long-eared brown bat on the hunt.

The Bat Incident

I'm too young to get a job but not too young to get work experience. Two years after the trip to the west coast, when I'm fourteen, Mom arranges for me to volunteer at the John Janzen Nature Centre in Edmonton. Once a week, we hop into the car for the 45-minute drive to the part of Edmonton where the Whitemud Creek drains into the North Saskatchewan River. The river valley is the largest stretch of parkland in any North American city. Plenty of wildlife lives here and sometimes people spot coyotes, deer, or even moose on city streets. I think it's kind of exciting for people but not so much for the animals. I wonder why they don't just stay away when they see city lights.

Inside the Nature Centre, displays show some of the animals that live in the river valley—bats, beavers, rabbits, skunks, and plenty of insects. My job is to help prepare materials for day camps, run the film projector, and answer visitors' questions. It's fun to tell people cool facts about animals. I like to point out that bats are the only mammals that can fly and bats don't just migrate, they hibernate, too. I think one day I might want a paying job that has something to do with wildlife. I imagine what it would be like to have my own nature center.

When my summer volunteering is over, I go to spend a weekend with my aunt and uncle near St. Paul so Mom and Dad can fly to Vancouver. My Mom grew up on this farm but in a different house. I try to imagine her as a kid. It's pretty tough because she hardly has any pictures of herself growing up.

I don't mind being left behind because I love the farm. It's a great place to look up at the stars. Sometimes I get to drive the lawn tractor

52

by myself. Even better is riding the horse, an old white mare named Pride. But this visit is the best, because my aunt lets me drive her car!

After supper on Saturday, Aunt Doris and I go to town to visit Grandma. The drive takes us past the world's first UFO Landing Pad. I can't tell you why the town built a landing pad for aliens. They just did. A wide set of stairs leads up to a giant, round, raised cement platform. Flags line the back and a sign says: *All visitors from Earth and elsewhere are welcome to the town of St. Paul.*

I wonder if there are other planets like Earth and whether people really do see lights in space that can't be explained any other way. I do know it's easier to see the night sky here than at home. It's so much darker away from big city lights.

Lots of stores would still be open in Sherwood Park right now. Here everything is closed except the gas stations, a convenience store, and a couple of bars. Even though the streets are dead, a neon sign flashes on a dark building: *Come in, we're open.* When we reach Grandma's neighborhood, I notice some houses have outdoor lights on even though the Sun is still far from setting. Maybe they leave them on to attract Martians.

After our visit, we head back toward the farm. We're cruising down a gravel road when Aunty turns to me and asks, "Do you want to drive?" I confess that I don't have my Learner's Permit yet and she says, "That doesn't matter."

So I say, "Okay!" and she pulls over. We switch places and she shows me how to adjust the seat. I take a deep breath, put my foot on the gas pedal, and the car leaps ahead. Panicking, I slam the brake so hard we nearly sail over the dashboard.

"Try again, nice and slow," says Aunt Doris. "Just ease up and down on the pedals."

I try again and the car shoots forward. Remember, this is in the days before people cared much about wearing seat belts. My aunt is a very brave woman. At first, I drive so slowly a kid on a bicycle could have passed us, but after a few kilometers of nothing going wrong, I speed up. We never see another car. That's a good thing because I feel like I need to be in the center of the road. I think I would hit the ditch if I had to move over even a foot. We reach the field where Uncle Ferna and my cousin Ron are baling hay, and I manage to park the car without hurtling us through the window.

"Thanks, Aunty," I say as we hop out of the car. I'm already planning in my head how I'm going to tell my sisters I know how to drive.

The next day is Sunday. Mom and Dad will be picking me up. During the afternoon, I'm reading at the kitchen table while Aunt Doris folds the laundry she just brought in from the clothesline. Turning a page, I look up to see her shake the wrinkles out of a pair of jeans and try to fold them flat. But something's stuck in the leg. "Probably a sock," she says to me, and gives the jeans a hearty snap. Out sails a little brown bat! Just like the ones I've been talking about all summer at the Nature Centre.

Aunty screams and dashes down the hall.

I don't know what to do. Has she gone to get my uncle? Is she coming back? The bat lands on the floor, then leaps into flight and circles around the room. It dodges the chandelier and cupboards and tall lamp, then shoots up to the ceiling where it hangs upside down, clinging to the white stipple. It looks like a mouse with wings.

Aunt Doris races back into the room,

carrying a blue plastic pail with dried white paint drips. I point to the ceiling. She drags a chair over, climbs up, and plops the pail over the bat.

"We need a piece of cardboard to slide under the bucket," she says. "Can you look in the drawer by the phone?" I find a pad of paper with cardboard in the back, peel it from the pad, and race back over to her. We both realize at the same time that she needs both hands to keep the bucket in place.

I drag another chair over and bit by bit slide the cardboard between the bucket and ceiling. Bits of stipple rain down on us. I feel the cardboard push up against the bat's tiny feet and stop. We look at each other. "He won't let go," I say but then I try again. Plunk! The bat lands in the pail.

We don't hear the car that drives into the yard and nearly drop the bat bucket when my parents walk into the kitchen. They stare at us standing up on the chairs.

"Did you spill something on the ceiling?" asks Dad.

"A bat came in on the laundry," I explain. "It's in the bucket." Mom backs down the hall.

Dad pounds on his chest and does his imitation of the Batman call. "Na, na, na, na, na, na na, na ... BATMAN!"

At that moment Uncle Ferna walks in. Dad stops imitating superheroes, Mom pretends it's not funny, and I laugh out loud. My aunt hands him the bucket and explains what happened.

"I'll never leave the laundry out overnight again," she exclaims. Uncle Ferna takes the pail to the barn and places it on a shelf where cats can't reach. He figures the bat will take off when it's dark. We check before leaving and, sure enough, it's gone.

Mexican long-tongued bat.

ARTIFICIAL LIGHT AND BATS

All bats are nocturnal and almost all insect-eating bats feed at night.

They capture insects and find their way using echolocation—a process of sending out high-pitched signals and listening for the sounds to return. Being active at night allows bats to avoid hawks and other birds of prey.

Bats' eyes are adapted for low-light conditions. Even small amounts of light can upset their natural behavior. Light interferes with foraging and makes it easier for predators to catch bats. Some bat species won't go near a light. Others circle streetlights to capture the insects that swarm there.

BATS THAT AVOID LIGHT

When not hibernating, bats spend their days in dark roosts. Trees, cliffs, rock crevices, bridges, and abandoned buildings are all safe places to hide. At dusk and dawn, bats leave their roosts to hunt. They need to build up fat for hibernation. The insects they eat are most plentiful during twilight.

Before leaving, some bat species go in and out of the roost several times to check light conditions. This behavior is called light sampling. When night reaches the right level of darkness, bats take off to hunt. If outdoor lights make night slow to get dark, bats delay leaving. As a result, they miss the best feeding time.

Outdoor lighting can cause bats to desert a roost. They may even leave an area in favor of darker locations. But sometimes light is everywhere. Rows of streetlights produce light barriers that bats will not cross. Bats do not always find other ways to reach feeding sites. Lights may also impact their movements when they try to migrate.

Bats traveling to feeding areas always use the same paths—called commuter routes. They follow rows of trees or shrubs, riverbanks, or canals. Bats use these landscapes for landmarks—to help find their way. Commuter routes also offer shelter from wind, habitat for foraging, and protection from predators. When outdoor lights pollute a commuter route, light-sensitive bat species stop using the pathway. Outdoor lighting makes the habitat unusable.

When winter comes, bats need to hibernate in dark, quiet places. Unfortunately, light can wake them up. Bats that are disturbed during hibernation may use up their fat supplies and not have enough energy to live until spring. Those that do survive may become less healthy.

BATS THAT GO TO LIGHT

Have you ever noticed moths and other insects gathered around outdoor lights? Next time you see bugs swarm around a light, look higher up. You may see bats circling above. These bats are not attracted to light. Instead, they come to catch insects flying around the light.

Bats follow each other to good feeding sites. This can lead to more bats gathering around lights than foraging in the surrounding habitat. Some bat species seem to prefer streetlights to unlit habitat. Moths are easier for bats to catch when both are near a light.

Are streetlights good for bats? No, lights interfere with normal bat behavior. Any interference with a species' natural behavior tends to have unwanted side effects. For example, light allows birds of prey and domestic cats to see bats. Predators are more likely to capture bats around lights at night.

BATS DESERVE YOUR LOVE

Why should you care about bats? One reason is they eat more night-flying insects than any other predator. One little brown bat can gobble up to 1,200 insects in one hour! Most insect-eating bats eat from 50 to 100 percent of their body weight every summer night. That's the same as a 30-kilogram (66 pound) person eating 15 to 30 kilograms (33 to 66 pounds) of food in one day! Bats save farmers a lot of money on pesticides.

Bats pollinate or disperse the seeds of more than 300 plant species, including bananas and avocados. Bat excrement, called guano, is used as a plant fertilizer. Scientists even study vampire bat spit. It contains a substance that stops blood from clotting. Researchers study this substance in hopes of using what they learn to develop drugs to help people who have strokes.

Following Moose

Years pass. I graduate from high school when I'm seventeen. It's time to decide on a career. Maybe I'll become an astronomer. But I love nature and wildlife, too. I decide to study ecology—a science that explores relationships between organisms and their environments. I hope this will help me get a job where I can work outside.

My school is called NAIT, which stands for the Northern Alberta Institute of Technology. It's totally different than high school. I'm treated like an adult. I like being surrounded by people who share my interest in the outdoors. It's not weird to like birds anymore.

Many of my courses are about animals or plants. I come to understand the difference between preserving the environment and conservation management. Humans need to coexist with nature. There is a need for places where the environment is untouched but there is also a need for places where people can get what they require from the planet without wrecking it.

One of my school projects involves writing a report based on new research. An instructor connects me with a group of people from the University of Alberta. They are studying moose behavior and need volunteers. If I help, they will share the results of their research. I agree.

It's a Saturday night in January. Two feet of snow cover the ground and the thermometer reads 23 degrees below Celsius. I'm at the Ministik Wildlife Research Station, a half-hour drive from Sherwood Park. The station is 65 hectares of aspen and boreal forest. I sit inside a dingy white and yellow Atco trailer as a researcher named Lyle explains the project.

He wants to understand the foraging habits of moose and figure out whether they use different habitats for resting and feeding.

The plan is to take turns following and recording the activity of a two-and-a half-year-old cow moose for a 24-hour period. She is fitted with a radio collar so we can locate her in the bush. A nine-foot fence borders part of the research park. Although the moose won't escape the enclosure, if she decides to run, I'll have to track her through the snow. Moose can be dangerous, especially during the breeding season or when a mother is protecting her calf. Around six feet tall at the shoulders, a female might weigh 350 kilograms. Luckily, this moose is semi-tame because she was hand-reared. We're not to pet her or get too close but we don't have to fear her either.

A volunteer in the trailer will write down all the observations. I'm expected to carry a baggy and pick up any moose droppings released on my shift. That could be a lot, considering a moose eats up to twenty kilograms of plant matter a day. The researchers will use a laboratory to analyze the droppings and learn about her diet. I'm glad my volunteering doesn't include working in the lab.

My shift isn't until midnight, so I lie down in a bunk and try to get comfortable. It's hard to sleep in a strange place. My eyes won't stay closed and I toss around. There are too many lights on and the radio crackles every few minutes. I can't turn off my mind. What will moose watching be like? Finally, the alarm on my watch tells me it's time for my two-hour shift.

I'm already wearing long johns (I call them "long joans"). I pull on my ski pants, down-fill jacket, toque, scarf, ski mitts, and white knee-high moon boots, then follow one of the researchers into the night to find the moose. He knows the area and leads me across a field and into the woods. The packed snow squeaks beneath our boots as we crunch along the twisting trail through trembling aspen and clumps of birch. We traipse on through the woods, taking a sudden right into a clearing.

A dark brown shape twitches an ear.

Wow! A moose is awfully massive this close up. Her muscled shoulders form a humped back and I can see her long legs are clearly built for getting through underbrush and deep snow. I step closer to look at the blue radio collar around the moose's neck, but it's her face that intrigues me. Something about her long mournful nose and donkey ears makes me feel I'm right where I belong. We're close enough to touch, but I control my urge to reach out a hand.

The volunteer at the end of his shift hands me the two-way radio and heads back to the trailer with the researcher. Just like that, I'm alone in the dark with a moose. The night is quiet. A half-moon shines through the trees and sparkles across the snow. Distant stars twinkle. Orion's belt shines through the bare tree branches. I feel calm because the sky helps me know where I am.

The moose looks at me for a moment, then turns her head toward the willow and begins to nip at the tips of the branches. I hold the radio to my lips, try to feel the talk button through my mitten, and report, "Moose browsing on willow." My breath forms a white cloud with each exhale. The moose exhales an even larger cloud of mist but I know she's not cold. Her winter coat is so thick that she'll be too hot if the temperature goes above minus-five degrees Celsius (23°F).

The moose steps along the willow scrub and leans down low. "Moose pawing ground and eating leaves." I stay about twenty feet behind my new friend and report every move. She nibbles dogwood, trembling aspen, and beaked hazelnut. Sometimes she raises her giant nose and sniffs the air, or pauses to chew her cud.

Every once in a while, my toque slips too far down my forehead and the warmth makes

THE INVISIBLE MILKY WAY
After lifetimes of gazing into the dark night sky, a point has come when many people can no longer see its wonders. Some have never glimpsed the arms of our galaxy—the Milky Way. Others have never seen a constellation, planet, comet, or star.

my glasses steam up. I'm peering through my foggy glasses when the moose stops eating and turns her head toward the direction of the trailer. Two brown ears go up. I report, "Moose alert."

This time a voice comes back to me. "Don't worry—Lyle just left the trailer. She'll know it's him and relax." Almost as soon as the radio crackle stops, the moose's ears go down.

"Moose at ease," I report but I can't believe it. We must be at least two kilometers away from the trailer! What incredible hearing! I feel so safe knowing my companion can hear from such a distance. Nothing is going to sneak up on us.

Then it happens. I bring the radio to my lips. "Moose dropping scat." I push my toque higher up my head and stoop down with my baggy. At least in winter there's little smell. Moose droppings are dry—so really not that disgusting. What's gross is putting the warm bag in my pocket. What if I forget to hand it over later and it drops out of my pocket in a store? I focus on remembering, keeping up

to the moose, and enjoying the dark night. I'm so glad the Ministik Wildlife Research Station exists. It's important to have places where animals can be observed in their natural habitat and places where the night sky is truly black.

LIGHTS OFF FOR PLANTS

Plants are vital parts of ecosystems and most life on Earth depends on plants for oxygen. From the smallest moss to the greatest tree, plants provide the habitat and food that moose and other plant-eating animals, called herbivores, need to survive. Meat-eating animals, known as carnivores, need plants, too, or there would be no prey for them to feed on. Plants reduce erosion, filter and purify water, and provide humans with a multitude of products including medicines, wood, paper, and rubber. Plants also absorb carbon, which in turn reduces global warming.

Unfortunately, artificial light at night can impact how well plants grow. Plants react to light intensity—how brightly light shines.

They also react to day length as it changes throughout the year. Day length is called photoperiod—the period of daylight within a cycle of light and dark.

Plants sense light through photoreceptors—special molecules that detect light. Photoreceptors enable plants to recognize whether it is spring or fall. They tell plants to grow during long summer days and drop their leaves when days shorten. Photoreceptors allow plants to do everything at the right time—grow flowers, release seeds, and enter dormancy—a resting period where growth stops until warmer or wetter weather returns.

Even though plants depend on light for life, they still need dark nights. A light shining into a forest, yard, or garden will impact some plant species. The light from streetlamps might cause some types of trees to drop their leaves at a different time than trees growing in dark areas. Some tree species respond by growing rapidly too late in the season. Late-growing twigs, branches, shoots, and roots often die when winter comes. Certain plants respond to artificial light as if two nights have passed instead of one. Artificial light can upset a plant's ability to flower or go dormant.

Light can also speed up a plant's life cycle, causing it to mature more quickly. This can cause problems for herbivores. They might run out of food if plants go through their life cycle too fast. If this happens, predators in the food chain will be affected next.

CHANGING DAY LENGTH

Like people, animals need to be ready for the changes that come in spring, summer, fall, and winter. Photoperiod and temperatures that increase or decrease tell animals the season is changing.

Animals have unique adaptations that

Ptarmigan in molt.

allow them to survive changing conditions. Each season brings different reactions. In spring, animals shed their warm winter coats and grow lighter ones to match the changing vegetation. Some birds respond by molting and growing new feathers as camouflage. Many animals breed in response to lengthening days.

Summer is spent raising young, growing, and putting on fat. Birds in temperate climates nest when day lengths are longest. In fall, animals adapt by getting ready for winter. Birds migrate. Moose, deer, and other animals that mate in the fall respond to shortening days. Some species, like snowshoe hare, grow a white coat to replace their brown fur. This camouflage helps them hide from coyotes and other predators that would otherwise spot them in snow.

Reindeer grow thicker coats, too. Light beige hair replaces the dark brown fur that keeps them hidden in summer. Tufts of hair grow between their hooves to prevent their footpads from freezing. As fall turns to winter, moose and other animals grow warm winter coats. Growing a thicker coat takes more energy, so moose need to eat more at this time of year.

Ptarmigans molt their brown summer feathers and grow white winter plumage. Other bird species, whales, insects, turtles, and fish migrate to places where food is more plentiful. Some animals hibernate. Others, like frogs, dig down into mud to become dormant until spring.

In winter, when less food is available, the short days trigger some animals to have less appetite. Certain species, like moose, reduce their activity to conserve energy. All these creatures depend on predictable periods of light and dark to trigger their seasonal adaptations.

Imagine living your whole life in the dark! Some animals are adapted to live with little or no light at all. They may be born in the permanent darkness of a cave or deep in an ocean. Some become blinded if exposed to light!

Working Outside

After two years, I graduate with a diploma in ecology. I find work as a park naturalist. Part of my job is to take people on hikes and teach them about plants and animals. It's fun.

Now I can spend a lot of time outside and stay up late to look at the night sky. I discover the Big Dipper becomes the Big Bear when it's dark enough to see the dimmer surrounding stars. I read astronomy books. I look at pictures taken through telescopes and see amazing images of nebulas, star clusters, and exploding stars called supernovas. The universe is endless. Scientists will never run out of things to discover. But I wonder if they can discover a solution to a problem that really bugs me—light pollution.

The more I stargaze, the more I notice how light it is at night. House lights, car lights, streetlights, skyscraper lights, signs with lights—it's everywhere! All that light makes it hard to see the stars. In some places, I can only see the brightest stars and closest planets. It makes me sad. At first, I think light pollution is just a problem for stargazers and astronomers. Then I discover light is a problem for animals and plants, too. Now I'm mad.

A NEW SCIENCE

I want to learn more about the importance of darkness. It turns out I'm not alone. Scientists want to understand why animals need dark, too. In 2003, they establish a new science called scotobiology. Its name comes from the old Greek work *skotos*, which means "for the dark." Scotobiology looks at how people, animals, and plants need darkness as part of their natural life

cycles. They are realizing that unwanted light at night affects animals, plants, and even humans.

LIGHT AND SMOG

At night, a naturally occurring chemical reaction reduces air pollution. A form of nitrogen oxide, called the nitrate radical, breaks down chemicals that form smog and ozone. The nitrate radical helps keep the air clean. Unfortunately, sunlight and light pollution destroy the radical. It only works at night. Light pollution makes air pollution last longer.

LIGHT POLLUTION AROUND THE PLANET

Unwanted light impacts you, no matter where you live. When the fossil fuels used to produce energy are wasted, a needless increase in greenhouse gases occurs. This contributes to global warming and climate change. The bulbs and light fixtures used to generate unwanted light are squandered,

too. They wear out more quickly and must be replaced more often, leading to increased garbage at landfill sites.

Lighting laws are designed to make sure people still have the light they need for safety and security. At the same time, these laws are meant to benefit the environment by stopping light from being directed into the sky or used in other wasteful, harmful ways. In Ontario, Central Manitoulin has bylaws that promote efficient outdoor lighting so that the night sky can still be seen. Many regions in Italy, as well as Slovenia, also have laws in place to regulate lighting. Unfortunately, most cities, communities, and countries do not have laws that regulate lighting or even guidelines to encourage the proper use of light.

Satellite measurements and pictures taken from outer space show that the irresponsible use of light occurs around the world. Changing the way people light their environments will involve international organizations, governments, engineers, and experts in lighting design, as well as astronomers and people concerned about nature. Governments that do make laws to ensure the responsible use of light will discover that their efforts save money, benefit the environment, and help restore the night sky to a place of awe.

ASTRONOMERS NEED DARK

The night sky provides our only view of the universe, but excessive light makes work difficult for professional astronomers who need very dark skies to see distant objects in outer space. Light pollution frustrates recreational stargazers and amateur astronomers, too. Amateurs often make discoveries that are important to science.

Astronomers have reacted to the problem by locating observatories in remote locations, but this solution is not ideal. Unwanted light is increasing as developing countries become wealthier and more people choose to live in cities.

Studying the night sky is important. Scientists watch for meteorites, asteroids, and comets that could hit the Earth. Discovering how stars behave helps us understand the closest star to Earth—our Sun. We need to know how the Sun behaves because it creates our weather. Its solar flares cause auroras and affect radio transmissions. The Sun and Moon create tides. Stars must be visible, too. They can be used for navigation. Constellations serve as a map of the sky, making it easier to describe where planets and other celestial objects are located. Studying planets teaches us about Earth and its atmosphere.

A NIGHT SKY FOR ALL

Scientists must be able to observe the night sky to advance science. All people deserve to be able to find places where they can look up at the night sky without interference from light pollution. Everyone deserves to enjoy the pleasures and excitement the night sky has to offer.

JET LAG

Have you ever flown in an airplane across a time zone? Traveling across multiple time zones in a short period can make you feel tired and irritable, a condition called jet lag. It occurs because photoreceptors in the brain of the air traveler must respond to sunlight at different times than they are used to. Over a couple of days, the body gradually adjusts to sunlight at the new time.

LIT UP!
Light pollution is most common in highly developed parts of the world—North America, Europe, Japan, and large cities in the Middle East and North Africa.

Dark Matters

Day and night reveal two different worlds. For most people, daytime is more familiar. Light makes us feel safe because we are most comfortable when we can see what is around us. Vision is our best sense and we rely upon it.

In true nighttime darkness, familiar landscapes change. The air feels different. Stars become visible. New sounds seem to emerge. The unknown creeps closer. It is natural to want to respond by turning on the lights.

People have only been able to turn on electric lights for just over 100 years. For the millions of years before that, animals and plants evolved in a cycle marked by both day and night. Our environment has not had enough time to adapt to light at night. And animals' natural behaviors are being impacted in ways we are only beginning to understand.

The use of artificial lighting has seemed harmless for a long time. Now scientists are discovering there is a cost to Earth's ecosystems. As animals and plants suffer, people will experience consequences, too. Scientists have a lot to learn in the science of scotobiology. As the importance of darkness becomes better understood, solutions to reduce human impact will become clearer. Fortunately it is easy to get started on reclaiming the night. Light pollution is one environmental problem where you can make an immediate difference.

SAVE THE DARK!
Write to people in your local and national governments. Ask them to:
* change lighting laws to protect habitat
* set up dark zones to decrease light pollution and save energy,
* establish preserves where people can view the dark sky.

What You Can Do

Light pollution is a problem that can be managed. You can help by using light in responsible ways and reminding others to do the same. When safety is not an issue, avoid using lights. If light is necessary, use the lowest wattage possible. Ensure light is only directed on the area that needs to be lit. It should not scatter in all directions or go up into the sky. Move lamps away from windows and close blinds at night to stop light trespass. Use timers and motion sensors to help ensure lights are only on when needed.

Turn off the lights for wildlife, plants, and for yourself. Enjoy the darkness and all the night has to offer. Look up at the stars, the planets, and our own Milky Way galaxy. Smell the white and yellow flowers opening their petals for nighttime pollinators. Listen to the owls. Try to spot a bat. Watch the fireflies flash their secret signals. The night is another world, only a light switch away.

MAKE A DIFFERENCE!

Learn more about how you can make a difference. Visit my website (www.joangalat.com) for activities and information relating to light pollution, or enter these search words into an Internet browser:

* Astronomy and light pollution
* Dark sky preserve
* Earth Hour
* Energy conservation
* Fatal Light Awareness Program (FLAP)
* Globe at Night
* International Dark-Sky Association (IDA)
* National Audubon Society in New York
* Royal Astronomical Society of Canada (RASC)
* Scotobiology

Credits